Black Panther

Story ARAVIND KRISH BALA   Pictures ASHOK RAJAGOPALAN

Tulika

My name is Veera and I know all the birds in the Anaimalai forests. I love birds, especially the great pied hornbills. I even showed their nests to Salim Ali, the birdman of India, many years ago. In return, he gave me his binoculars. I was 15.

That was a long time ago and I have many stories about the animals and birds I have seen in these forests. Tigers, elephants, gaurs…

But the best story of all is the one about the black panther.

My forefathers and elders in the village had talked about a black beast that roamed in the forest. But no one had seen it.

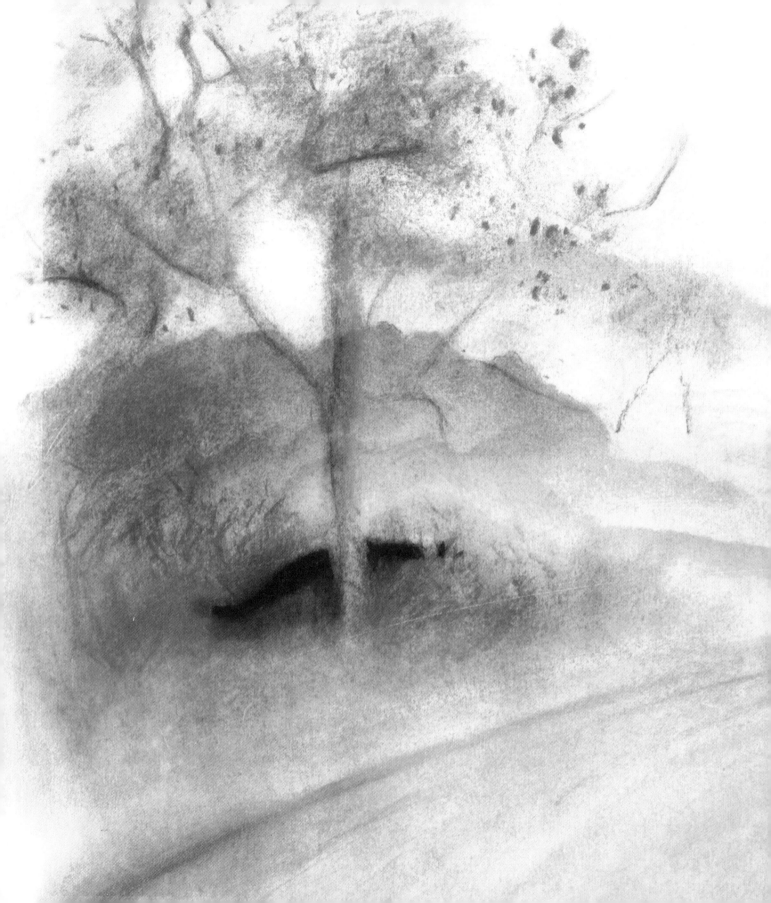

One day, my 11- year-old son Kari said he had spotted a big, black cat in the thorny bushes near a red silk cotton tree in the first bend up the hill.

I knew it was a black panther. I was thrilled.

So, I began spending my evenings under that red silk cotton tree. Kari waited with me on Saturdays and Sundays.

For 22 days we had no luck.

One day, while we waited, we watched herds of
elephants migrating down a familiar path from one
forest to another. We spotted sambars, jackals and
a leopard.

I had seen all these in the wild many, many times.
My heart was beating for the black panther.

Another morning, we saw a tigress with two cubs.

That evening, we were sitting by the side of the narrow, winding hill road, when lightning struck. The last bus had rattled past half-an-hour ago. The forest was still. And then…

We could not believe our eyes!

There came the black panther, walking majestically beneath the red silk cotton tree on to the road. He was a brilliant black.

He looked on both sides like a schoolboy trying to cross the road, and stretched. Then he growled and lay down right in the middle.

He yawned and went to sleep as the sky drizzled golden drops of rain.

Kari and I wanted to have a closer look. I moved across the road. Kari stayed where he was.

Like the panther, we lay down and slowly rolled towards him from either side.

We were about ten feet from him when he jumped up, smelling us.

We were terrified. I motioned to my son to stay still.

Thankfully, the panther was not looking at Kari. Grumbling deeply, he walked towards me with soft, sure steps. Holding my breath, I prayed to all my forefathers.

I could see the hexagonal patterns on his sleek, black body. His thick, long tail bunched at the tip.

As he came closer, he sniffed me. His reddish tongue was hanging out, his teeth were like small, sharp, ivory nails. Inside those yellow eyes, two black marbles shone.

Then, slowly, the magnificent black cat started licking me.

Suddenly, Kari jumped up and shouted wildly.
He vowed to grab the panther by his tail and fling
him far away.

Surprised by the noise, the panther was confused.

Now I knew I had a chance. I jumped up and shouted at the black panther: "How dare you lick me?"

Slowly, the panther began to back away from us. He stared at us all the while with his cold, terrifying eyes before vanishing into the scrub jungle. It looked like he was telling us that he would have his day.

The sun was about to set in all its splendour and it began to drizzle again. The rain god took out his colourful bow. Flocks of birds swept over the cliff like crisp arrows.

Kari and I walked back home along the winding ghat road singing and dancing with joy. We had seen a black panther!